HOW TO FART
AT WORK

D1464859

To all the office workers stuck in non-air-conditioned lifts.

"When the thunderclap comes, there is no time to cover the ears."
Sun Tzu, The Art of War

THIS IS A CARLTON BOOK

Published by Carlton Books Ltd
20 Mortimer Street
London W1T 3JW

Text copyright © 2019 Mats and Enzo
Design copyright © 2019 Carlton Books Ltd

A CIP catalogue for this book is available from the British Library.

Designer: Harj Ghundale
Art Editor: Andri Johannsson
Project Editor: Chris Mitchell
Production: Jessica Arvidsson

ISBN 978-1-78739-305-9

Printed in China

10 9 8 7 6 5 4 3 2 1

HOW TO FART
AT WORK

MATS & ENZO

CARLTON
BOOKS

CONTENTS

Introduction   6
The Expert: Tom Hayatt   11

**Chapter 1: The Physics and the Anatomy of
Farting at Work**
A natural but little known and unwelcome
    phenomenon in companies   13
The propagation of odour: "Why is the smell
    following me?"   14
Spreading from an office chair   16
Free spread in a group of individuals   17
Understanding the BFS   18

Chapter 2: Basic Skills
Murphy's laws of flatulence   20
The golden rules of farting at work   20
Never use these six techniques to fart at work!   21
The Plan-Check-Release (PCR) method   22
Know when an opportunity to relieve
    yourself arises   23
Where to fart at work   24
How to break wind in your own office   25
Skills you must know if you work in an open-
    plan office: the coffee trick   26
Purifying morning exercises: get rid of
    stomach gases at home, not at work!   27
How to fart in a lift at work   28
Never fart in a lift going down   29
When can I fart safely in the stairwell?   30
Can I fart during a business meeting?   31

Chapter 3: Problematic Situations
Common problems encountered when farting
    at work   32
The dangers   33

You let one rip very loudly in your
    open-plan office   34
It's a stinker   36
You are having a bad day in your
    open-plan office   38
You are being summoned, but you can't get up   40
You sit down and your chair makes a
    farting noise   42
The air conditioning in your open-plan office
    is broken, and the building smells rotten   44
Alone in your cubicle, you fart, but someone
    arrives at that moment   46
You fart at the end of the corridor, when
    someone arrives   48
You are walking towards the toilet and
    someone notices your peculiar behaviour   50
Your boss is walking behind you   52
You fart during the ride and someone enters   54
You enter the lift and the smell in it is horrific 56
You enter the lift with several other people,
    and the smell is unbearable   58
You need to break wind, but there are several
    others in the lift   60
The lift breaks down. You and your colleagues are
    stuck in it for three hours   62
Your boss farts next to you   64
You are making noise in your stall   66
The person in the neighbouring stall is relieving
    himself loudly, which makes you freeze   68
You are making noise, and someone calls
    you from outside   70
You are using the urinal next to a colleague,
    and you accidentally let one rip   72
You leave the toilet and your clothes smell
    very bad   74

You stink up a stall and leave just as a
   colleague enters 76
You let out a noisy one during an
   important meeting 78
You let out a smelly one during an
   important meeting 80
You are in the middle of a presentation 82
Someone farts and everyone looks at you 84
You let out a stinker and people leave
   in outrage 86
You stuffed your face during a company
   breakfast and you feel bloated 88
You let out a stinker next to the photocopier just
   as a colleague arrives 90
Your office stinks 92
You break wind just as someone enters
   your office 94
You simply must fart, but your boss won't
   leave your office 96
Your colleague breaks wind in your office 98
You are alone in your office and you fart. The
   smell becomes unbearable 100
You are spraying air freshener when your
   boss enters 102
You let rip such a noisy one that people in
   the hallway can hear you 104
The office cafeteria goes vegan 106
The moment you stink up the smoking room,
   your boss arrives for a smoke 108
You are outside with a group of colleagues
   and you let one rip 110
You fart loudly in your boss's office 112
You let out a stinker in your boss's office 114
Your boss is an incorrigible farter; you
   don't want to go to his office anymore 116
You share a hotel room with a colleague 118
You are in the car with your boss and
   you release a smelly fart 120
You are in the car with your boss and
   he farts 122
You are in the first row at a lecture and
   you interrupt the CEO by farting 124
You fart and the microphone picks it up 126
You stand up to ask a question, with dire
   consequences 128

Chapter 4: Farting Your Way to the Top
How to discredit your colleagues and boss by
   farting at work 131
Destabilization technique #1: The
   poisoned mug 132
Destabilization technique #2: Farting in
   a group 134
Destabilization technique #2: The office
   smells bad 136

Conclusion
Fart at Work: Looking for testimonials 139
BFS: first aid – Dr Smith's advice 142

You have chosen to acquaint yourself with flatulence at work. Good plan! Companies are governed by strict, all too often untold rules of conduct. Emitting loud smelly farts at work is never a good idea for job progression.

In 2009, we were the first look into the problems encountered by employees in company toilets, and the first to suggest solutions to them in our bestseller *How to Poo at Work*. It is with this same pioneering spirit that we now dive into the matter of workplace flatulence. Before we begin, you should know that another title for this oeuvre could be *How Not to Fart at Work* or *How to Hold in a Fart at Work* or perhaps *How to Avoid Getting Blamed for Farts at Work*.

Considering the global success of our previous work, we consider ourselves to have enough authority to break this new taboo and muddy the waters again by publishing a book that will once more create a stir and provoke debate.

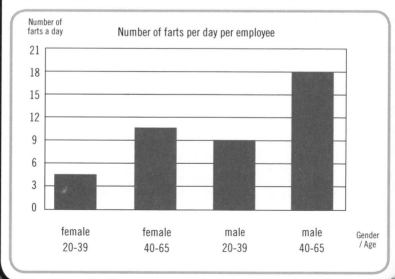

Before diving into this astonishing new book, have a look at the shocking numbers that speak much, much louder than the hushed tones we tend to use when approaching this subject. Our studies in 445 different companies show that each employee lets it rip between 8 and 15 times each day during office hours. You (yes, you; let's stop pretending), your office mate, your colleagues in accounting, the receptionist, your boss, your smartly dressed colleague in PR that you have always admired... We can now prove to you that all these people, whom you run into every single day at work, fart between 8 and 15 times per day.

We then made some spreadsheets and calculated annual values to help us understand the magnitude of the problem. On average, a company employs 154 people. That amounts to an amazing daily fart figure of between 1,232 and 2,310 in a single company. That's an average. In larger companies, the number of backdoor breezes may exceed 30,000, and can even go up to 50,000 gas attacks per day when beans are served in the canteen!

But back to you, who produces between 8 and 15 farts per day at work, and over 150,000 throughout your career. You, who must come up with a solution to this problem all by yourself every single time. Think about it: this means 150,000 complex situations in which you and every other employee around the globe must attempt to find a solution in a few seconds so as your colleagues or bosses

Rest assured that all employees encounter the same problems as yourself, but nobody dares break the code of silence on this particular subject. All your colleagues behave as if this loud and smelly problem doesn't exist or affect them at all.

Yet the evidence is everywhere:

• A colleague comes out of the lift and seems unhappy to see you. When you enter the lift, you smell why.
• A teammate jumps from his seat suddenly and leaves hastily, as if to attend to something important, but within a minute returns empty-handed.
• Your boss starts talking to you, then begins to fidget and leaves quickly.
• After two hours of meetings, conference rooms smell as if something died in them.

How, we ask, is it possible that nobody has come up with any intelligent solutions for these situations?

- Has any manager under the sun ever organized a long, all-hands meeting to discuss the farting and possible solutions?
  No.
- Have you ever participated in a farting brainstorm?
  No.
- Have you received an email outlining guidelines or best practices on farting at work?
  No.
- Has anyone thought to put an air freshener in the corner of the lift?
  No.
- Is there a soundproofed and ventilated room in your workplace for farting, just as there is for smoking?
  No.

don't hear or smell you. Each of you poor souls must evaluate in a split second if what is coming will be noisy, smelly, or both, and find a way to deal with the consequences of this physiological problem, which can become, at the very least, extremely embarrassing, or worse, ruin your reputation and entire career.

In your workplace, as in so many others, the problem of farts is completely overlooked; until now, employees have been left to their own devices when facing thousands of situations each year in which they most certainly don't want to be caught. This is a major source of stress that is never considered when researching the effects of stress at work.

Let's look at what is really at stake here. A lone careless moment or poorly estimated fart trajectory, volume or odour can annihilate a flourishing career. We all know what happens. You only need to get caught twice to be nicknamed "Mr Fartypants" and become the colleague we all laugh at when he's not around, the employee nobody sits next to in the canteen, and the one who mysteriously never gets a promotion...

Mankind has made incredible progress through its capacity of new shared knowledge. But the apparent gag order on the subject of flatulence has kept it in the shadows. New discoveries in office farting techniques have never been shared, leaving hardworking men and women everywhere to their own devices.

If you are familiar with our work, which is scientific, methodical and very innovative, you will know that we work tirelessly on the solutions to real problems that are regularly encountered in the workplace, but which are too often overlooked or completely ignored. This time is no different. We have devoted hundreds of days (even months!) to tests and experiments in big companies in order to come up with techniques that work when the urge to fart at work overcomes you.

As with *How to Poo at Work*, we collaborated with Tom Hayatt, the world-renowned expert on all tricky situations stemming from the digestive tract of the modern worker.

Do not think for a second that we are not aware how controversial this book is. Some of our techniques will disturb certain people. But we also know that this book will immediately find its place among the greatest management manuals of all time. It will proudly stand on the shelves of business schools at Harvard, Stanford and Oxford, and probably appear on the cover of *Time*. It will also stand side by side with works such as Warren Bennis's *On Becoming a Leader*, Daniel Goleman's *Emotional Intelligence*, Sheryl Sandberg's *Lean in*, or *Built to Last: Successful Habits of Visionary Companies* by Jim Collins and Jerry Porras.

We also know that this book will often be mistakenly placed on the shelves marked "Humour" in bookstores by staff members who don't know any better for reasons that you surely understand by now. They simply will not see that the book they hold in their hands is the very solution to the problem they also face every single day at work. But we are willing to live with this insult if it means that it will bring our book closer to as many readers as possible. This has already happened with *How to Poo at Work* and contributed to its record-breaking success.

But there is nothing funny about this book. We are publishing it because we believe it is high time the difficult subject of breaking wind at work is taken seriously. No more ruined careers because of one innocent lunch at a Mexican restaurant, or nascent gastroenteritis, or failure to control a flatus that announced itself to be much more innocent than it was!

We have the solutions, and we want to share them with you.

The book you hold in your hands will give you a better understanding of a complex issue, which links medicine, aerodynamics, social psychology and management. You will discover our proven techniques. Never again will you find yourself at a loss after accidentally breaking wind in the company lift or your open-plan office, or when an inconsiderate colleague expunges their intestinal gas in your office.

Understanding air phenomena linked to flatulence, knowing how to prevent them, choosing your meals at the cafeteria well... We have worked tirelessly on such subjects for five years to bring you advice that we haven't found anywhere else.

As any good management book will tell you, any problem can become an opportunity. See the last chapter entitled "Fart your way to the top", which includes step-by-step guidance on using flatulence to boost your career.

Our books are heavy with information and, as with our previous work, one read-through will not be enough to absorb the entirety of our brilliant solutions. You should memorize each of these techniques and practice at home before applying them at work. Have a family member repeat them with you.

No employee should let flatulence ruin their career. We fight this battle alongside you through this book: together, we will prevail.

MATS & ENZO

THE EXPERT: TOM HAYATT

Tom Hayatt is an indisputable authority on the subject of toilets in the workplace. It was he who first shed light on the issue in the prestigious Management Journal of the Massachusetts Institute of Technology in a 1987 article, "Real Social Working Dynamics for Water Closets". At first, he was not taken seriously. But in 1992 he was finally recognized by his peers, especially because of the prestigious award given to him that same year: the Golden Toilet Brush. His name was even circulated for a while as a possible candidate for the Nobel Prize in Economy.

Tom Hayatt soon realized that he would have to research the second major subject matter that no other management book had tackled: farting at work. With the perfect combination of ambition and drive, Tom Hayatt then developed – without taking away from his research on workplace toilets – a new branch of expertise: the art of the business fart.

He invested millions into olfactory trials, in which he used company employees as guinea pigs and studied them in thermo-acoustic chambers. He was able to identify all the olfactory elements of farts emitted in confined spaces, as well as their sound spectrum, their speed and the timing of their ejections. (The Japanese anemometers he used recorded speeds of up to 174 km/h).

As always in his research, Tom Hayatt made it personal. He embarked on a strict but effective diet to generate gas: dinners of string beans, breakfast smoothies made with 1 kg of cabbage, 2 litres of fermented goat milk and 20 centilitres of fish oil. On top of his diet, he wore trousers a size too small. He produced between 50 and 80 farts per day throughout his seven-month testing period in various companies. He gathered 542 Gb of data on rectal gas and filled 12 notebooks with all sorts of observations and detailed technical sketches. These notebooks are now stored in the MIT library.

Yes, Tom Hayatt is ahead of his time. He has honoured us once again by sharing his rich theoretical and practical knowledge with us for this book: a perfect complement to our own methodologies and analyses. We thank him – as will you after reading this book – for unveiling his valuable solutions, which will undoubtedly help boost your career.

Indeed, in the last section of this book, Tom Hayatt will explain how an employee can be given new responsibilities if he becomes particularly adept at farting in the workplace. Tom Hayatt himself successfully rose from simple trainee to CEO of a multinational company by farting and pooing his way to the top.

Read on and learn how to follow the same fast track! **The advice of Tom Hayatt has changed our lives, and it is now about to change yours.**

If you don't follow the advice of Tom Hayatt, your career path will almost certainly continue to follow the blue line below. It is time to make the wise move.

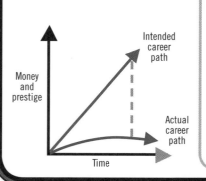

"How can a man take on new responsibilities if he struggles to fart at work? It does not matter how high or low on the career ladder you are, if you haven't trained to fart properly, getting a promotion will prove difficult, if not impossible."
Tom Hayatt

CHAPTER 1: THE PHYSICS AND THE ANATOMY OF FARTING AT WORK

A natural but little known and unwelcome phenomenon in companies

The phenomenon of flatulence is a subject that many think they know well, but when we were talking to employees in countless companies while doing research for this book, we established that, at best, most of them had only a rudimentary comprehension of this subject.

Many employees told us that they still referred to what their parents had told them on this strange airborne phenomenon. The more curious ones searched in old encyclopaedias or Wikipedia, but always failed to get past the first three paragraphs before having a laughing fit provoked by the descriptions of the genesis of flatulence or the pathologies linked to flatulence, such as aerophagia, ventosity, meteorism, bloating...

It became clear to us that we simply must begin this book with some physiological, medical and scientific information on farting.

THE PROPAGATION OF ODOUR: "WHY IS THE SMELL FOLLOWING ME?"

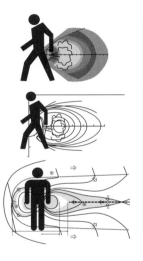

Stomach gases are the same temperature as the inside of your body (around 37°C). This means that they are typically warmer than the air in air-conditioned offices. As is the case with all warm gases, they rise when released, but they also quickly cool down. They gas reaches its final height (beyond which they stop rising) at about 165cm, which is exactly the average height of the nose of someone standing in an office.
It is also at this height that a circular aerodynamic current is then created.
(See head-convection illustration.)

Scientists at MIT have developed the model of this phenomenon, called the "Law of the flatulent fixation", with the following formulas:

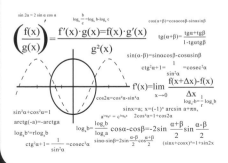

DIFFUSION

14

Let us explain. A fart emerges from its source at 37°C. Two flows are emitted. The first, called "the primary flow", cools off while it moves upwards. A vortex is then created, circling the fart around the head — and therefore, also the nose — of its creator, making them feel like they are trapped in or followed by the horrendous smell.

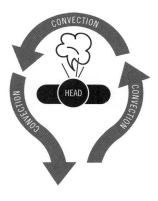

The second flow, called "the secondary flow", is slower but stronger. It rotates around the fart-maker and spreads towards people in their vicinity according to the laws of spreading, which we will now explain.

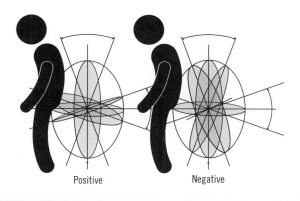

Positive   Negative

SPREADING FROM AN OFFICE CHAIR

"How much time does one have before being identified by their interlocutor as guilty of farting?"

3.12 seconds

2.03 seconds

1.13 seconds

0.23 seconds

Flatulence propagation/s $= \dfrac{R_s}{1 - (p \cdot psat/p) \cdot (1 - R_s/R_v)}$

We would like to thank MIT for lending us its sensor room. This is what we have discovered:

- If your colleague is in front of your desk, you have 3.12 seconds before they realize you farted.
- If your colleague is behind you — for example, when he or she is helping you with a spreadsheet or written correspondence — you have 1.13 seconds before they realize that you farted.

We advise you to always face your colleagues. This will give you precious seconds after you fart that you can use to get them to leave your office or set in motion one of the other powerful techniques from this book.

This study concerned only silent flatulence. Sound travels at 340.29 m/s. To put it differently: if you make a noise, your colleague will know immediately. Hence the importance of training at home to release silent farts.

FREE SPREAD
IN A GROUP OF INDIVIDUALS

This formula **FINALLY** gives a scientific frame to the problem we all encounter. How much time do we have before other members of the group realize that we have let our intestinal gas loose? We would again like to thank the people at MIT for making their sensor room available to us in order to conduct our research.

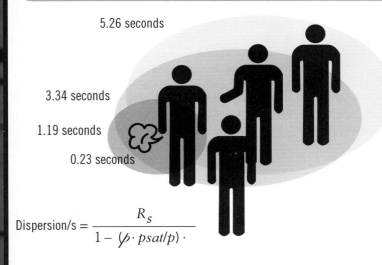

5.26 seconds

3.34 seconds

1.19 seconds

0.23 seconds

$$\text{Dispersion/s} = \frac{R_s}{1 - (p \cdot psat/p) \cdot}$$

In a group situation, where the issuer inadvertently lets loose a silent and smelly flatulence, he has only a short time before his colleagues (also referred to as "receptors") understand what has just happened.

In this situation, it takes only 3.34 seconds for two co-workers located less than 2 meters away to be overwhelmed by the smell. The thought of leaving the area will occur to them very quickly.

UNDERSTANDING BFS

Meetings, brainstorming, presentations to the board of directors, job interviews, annual reviews... The professional environment is full of situations in which an employee will feel trapped when the urge to relieve themselves of some gastric gases overcomes them.

0h   **3h**   **5h**   **8h**

From a medical point of view, the gases should be expunged immediately. They can be held in for a few seconds at best. Holding them in should certainly not become a habit because it can lead to serious long-term problems.

What happens to your body in an office?
If you hold in several successive farts, your body will soon suffer from BFS (Belly Fart Syndrome). In most cases, a worker will suffer simple bloating, but doctors tell us that it can lead to internal micro tears. We chose not to study this particular subject any further.

Use our techniques to no longer suffer from BFS.

Just as you wouldn't go deep-sea diving without at least some basic knowledge, you can't start farting like a pro at work without preparation. We will, therefore, begin with basic concepts that you should already know. Unfortunately, even though all employees must relieve themselves of gas several times per day, there is a total lack of company training dedicated to the subject.

We know that a slide presentation on farting, like the one you see above, has likely never taken place at your company – and that is why we wrote this book.

In the following pages you will discover that you have made mistakes when farting at work. However, there's no need to dwell on your past slip-ups. By deciding to read this book, you have made an important, life-changing decision. With its help, you will, from now on, properly manage the way you fart at work and, with that, will be able to take control of your entire career!

"The top people in the biggest companies are, unsurprisingly, often the best at farting in them. You can rest assured that they got where they are because they worked hard to excel in farting at work." - Tom Hayatt

Murphy's laws of flatulence

1. It comes out noisy when you are certain there was no way it would or could.
2. It stinks when you thought it wouldn't smell.
3. When you are alone and you fart, someone inevitably walks in.
4. The smell follows you exactly when it really shouldn't.
5. When holding it in, there is always someone preventing you from leaving.
6. The desire to fart always comes at the least convenient moment.
7. The smell goes towards people, rather than empty space in the room.

The golden rules of farting at work

Farts at the workplace are governed by nine clear rules. Even if they have never been written or formally defined, everyone must follow these rules. You can never break them, whatever the situation.

1. Never say: "It wasn't me!" = NEVER NOT GUILTY
2. Never say sorry. = NO EXCUSES
3. Never show emotions. = NO EMOTION
4. Do not change your demeanour. = NO CHANGE
5. If seated, never lean to the side to lift a buttock. = NO BUTTOCKING
6. Do not inhale through the nose with an air of satisfaction. = NO SNIFFING
7. Don't pass gas when there are only two of you present. = NO DEATH DUEL
8. Always be the first to point out a bad odour. = BE FIRST
9. Don't point out to others that they have broken wind. = BE GENTLE*

Unless you can use it for the advancement of your career.

"What is the recipe for achievement? To my mind, there are just four essential ingredients: Choose a career you love. Give it your very best. Seize your opportunities. And be good at farting at work. I believe you are one of the people who are able to fulfil all four of these requirements." - Tom Hayatt

NEVER USE THESE SIX TECHNIQUES TO FART AT WORK!

Whether it's during a conversation at the coffee machine, in the corridor or standing in your office, you should never use any of the following techniques. Everybody knows them, and you'll be fooling no one.

THE PLAN-CHECK-RELEASE (PCR) METHOD

With Tom Hayatt, we invented a special method that will help you fart at work. Carefully field-tested over a period of ten years, this method will enable you to discharge at work with minimal risk. It is of crucial importance that you apply this procedure prior to each fart.

Important Note: Even though you will eventually have used our techniques on over 3,500 farts per year, keep in mind that dangers lurk everywhere. No employee – expert or beginner – will avoid them if they don't respect the process.

"Never get overconfident about farting at work!" - Tom Hayatt

When you feel the need to expel gas, you need to use this method. By practising and perfecting the "PCR method" you will be able to fart at work successfully.

Plan: Define the execution precisely, especially the place of release. Don't forget to also work out how to exit the premises as quickly as possible.
Check: Make sure your mission is truly feasible in your current environment (colleagues nearby, functioning air conditioning, noise levels in the room…).
Release: Complete your mission and exit the zone.

Expert opinion

This simple method can save reputations at work! You should be systematic and apply yourself so as not to put your career in danger, but rather advance on your road to the top.

KNOW WHEN AN OPPORTUNITY TO RELIEVE YOURSELF ARISES

Relieving yourself at work without danger is possible when three important elements come together. This is your opportunity. It is illustrated in this diagram, which explains how to identify a favourable situation to execute your release.

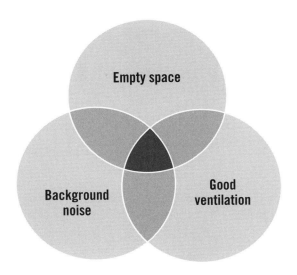

Great opportunity to fart at work

Risky opportunity

WHERE TO FART AT WORK

Step 1: Go quickly to the nearest safe space

Step 2: Keep calm and fart in peace

Use one of these very efficient sphincter positions which are recommended by doctors specializing in medicine at work as ideal for farting.

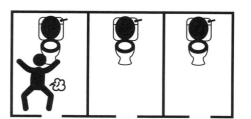 

HOW TO BREAK WIND IN YOUR OWN OFFICE

If you think that not sharing an office with anyone eliminates all dangers, you haven't given the situation enough thought – or perhaps you like to live dangerously.

For the release, you have two choices:

1. Stay at your desk and lift your leg.   2. Move and lift your leg.

The second technique is the best because it is often less noisy. We also strongly recommend that you think before acting. You should always anticipate the event of a person entering your office the second after you have dropped a bomb. Consider farting in a corner of your office where nobody goes, and hope that your fart will stay there.

SKILLS YOU MUST KNOW IF YOU WORK IN AN OPEN-PLAN OFFICE: THE COFFEE TRICK

1. You work at your desk and you feel that a fart is coming.
2. Stand up gently and walk to the bathroom SLOWLY to avoid an unexpected and premature release.
3. Release your fart quickly without being noticed by positioning your legs and your body in a way that limits noise.
4. Go to the coffee machine.
5. Come back to your desk with your coffee in hand. Drink your coffee at your desk and look around in a way that suggests you simply went for coffee and not for a massively smelly stink torpedo.

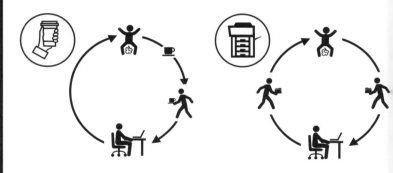

Naturally, you will not be able to drink between 8 and 15 coffees per day just to release your typical daily quota of farts. Be imaginative. A trip to the photocopier will work just as well. True, the warm air around the machine will amplify the odour, but you will be far away by then. It will no longer be your problem.

PURIFYING MORNING EXERCISES: GET RID OF STOMACH GASES AT HOME, NOT AT WORK!

The more you fart at work, the more you risk being caught and thus losing your credibility with your colleagues or your boss. It's crucial that you evacuate as much of your stomach gas as possible at home.

We have developed two pre-office techniques. The first one should be done in your home, and the other on your drive to work. Our exercises will assist the evacuation of around 2 to 7 farts each morning.

The Home Yoga Fart

Important: Do not attempt this exercise if you are expecting someone to arrive at any minute, or in the vicinity of your family when unsuspectingly enjoying their breakfast. This basic exercise should be done in the morning. Repeat until all farts have exited your body.

Yoga Car Fart

Important: Open the windows or boost the air conditioning. For obvious security reasons, do not perform this exercise will driving, but only when stopped at a traffic light or in a traffic jam. Put both legs on the dashboard and hold the steering wheel firmly with both arms. Pull the steering wheel toward you while flexing your legs. This exercise is an excellent addition to the Home Yoga Fart, or its substitute if you are in a hurry.

HOW TO FART IN A LIFT AT WORK

We will now explain why you often feel the need to let rip when the lift goes up and not when it goes down.

You have undoubtedly noticed that you or your colleagues fart more often in the lift and that nobody knows how to handle this embarrassing situation. No scientist has yet been able to explain why we fart more when we are in a lift. However, the reason should be clear to anyone who took physics at school. With altitude, the change in air pressure must be equalized.

Did you know?

9% of farts in the workplace are released in lifts

NEVER FART IN A LIFT GOING DOWN

As the illustration shows, when a fart is released, it will first slowly rise as the lift goes down. A few floors later, it will reach nose level. Your fellow passengers will immediately realize what has happened and seek out the guilty party. If there are only two of you in the lift, the culprit will not be difficult to find.

Be careful in a lift going up

Breaking gas in a lift going up isn't safe either. If the flatulence is pushed to the ground on release because of the lift's upward motion, the fart will immediately rise again when the lift stops (the law of inertia). Only a swift exit from the lift could potentially save you, but your hurried movements and the lingering odour will leave no doubt to those remaining in the lift as to who let it rip.

Lifts are now increasingly fast. Doctors specializing in medicine at work are detecting more troubles related to flatulence in employees who work in high-rise buildings. We should also note that the engineers who conceived these super-fast lifts failed to realize that going from 0 to 650 metres above ground level in 7 seconds would surely provoke pressure adjustment *somewhere*.

WHEN CAN I FART SAFELY IN THE STAIRWELL?

If someone is following you down the stairs, do not fart!
You *must* hold it in.

If you pass a colleague or the manager of the company on the stairs, you must wait at least two steps before you break wind (according to our tests). If you fart at the moment you pass someone, they will sniff out the culprit.

Danger zone | Safety zone

CAN I FART DURING A BUSINESS MEETING?

This flow chart will help you make the right decision.

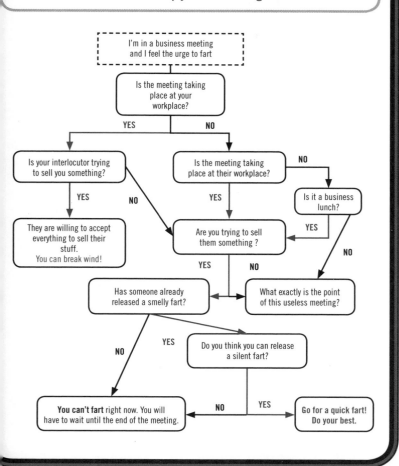

I'm in a business meeting and I feel the urge to fart

Is the meeting taking place at your workplace?

YES — **NO**

Is your interlocutor trying to sell you something?

YES — **NO**

They are willing to accept everything to sell their stuff.
You can break wind!

Is the meeting taking place at their workplace?

NO

Is it a business lunch?

YES — **NO**

Are you trying to sell them something ?

YES — **NO**

Has someone already released a smelly fart?

YES — **NO**

What exactly is the point of this useless meeting?

Do you think you can release a silent fart?

NO — **YES**

You can't fart right now. You will have to wait until the end of the meeting.

Go for a quick fart!
Do your best.

CHAPTER 3: PROBLEMATIC SITUATIONS

Common problems encountered when farting at work

This chapter will help you understand and avoid common pitfalls. We are your trustworthy and knowledgeable coaches, who will guide you through all the fart issues you could ever encounter throughout your career. Your farts will soon no longer be an obstacle to reaching the career heights you deserve. To keep this promise, we will reveal to you our original approach to give you solutions to every fart dilemma. We will tackle all situations – even the particularly tricky ones – and divulge all our techniques to help you survive risky situations. Each situation also comes with an expert opinion given by Tom Hayatt to further help your studies.

THE DANGERS

Every problem in this chapter is inspired by real events.
The key below will help identify potential pitfalls with the following
problematic scenarios.

Being heard

Being criticized

Bad smell

Being ashamed

Being seen

Being fired

PROBLEM: You let one rip very loudly in your open-plan office

OPEN-PLAN
OFFICE

You are seated comfortably at your desk when you feel a rectal tremor coming. Thinking you can control its release, you let it out. You assumed wrong. The fart is loud, and many colleagues around you automatically look up to see who did it.

Potential Dangers

SOLUTION: The sniper

1. You must act quickly.
2. Pick the nearest colleague. Paul, for example.
3. Stand up and say loudly: "Seriously, Paul! You're not at home watching telly with your wife!"
4. Taken by surprise, Paul will say it wasn't him.
5. Finish the take-down by saying: "And it's a stinker on top of it!"
6. Leave the office.

Expert opinion

If, like me, you have a room deodoriser in your desk drawer, stand up and calmly spray your nearest colleague without saying a word. All your colleagues in the open-plan office will know who to look at with their accusatory eyes.

Testimonial

I wanted to use this method, but a colleague raised a buttock, winking at me as if to say: "Nicely done, brother!" Because of this idiot, there are now two of us that our colleagues call Mr Fart.

Daniel, 40, IT support technician

PROBLEM: It's a stinker

OPEN-PLAN OFFICE

You are sitting at your desk and you let one go without making a sound. The bad news: it stinks horribly. The smell is unbearable and spreads around you like a plague.

Potential Dangers

SOLUTION: The focus

1. It is very difficult to know precisely who farted in an open-plan office. You simply need to stay calm. (To achieve this, avoid using the breathing technique where you relax by inhaling deeply through the nose before exhaling through the mouth.)
2. Avoid making eye contact with your colleagues. The panic in your eyes will betray you. Focus your eyes on any object in front of you. "Look, a blue pencil..."
3. It might seem interminable, but don't forget, a smell always dissipates in the end.
4. Don't take any more chances. This is not the day to break wind at the office one more time.

Expert opinion

Personally, I am never surprised by what I produce. I test the smell each morning to know what I should expect during the day.

Testimonial

I didn't know this technique at the time. I took a folder and waved it in the air to dissipate the smell. Bad call... It went instead in the direction of my boss, who was sitting about 10 metres away from me.

Ben, 24, archivist

PROBLEM: You are having a bad day in your open-plan office

OPEN-PLAN OFFICE

You arrived at your office only 30 minutes ago and you've already had to relieve yourself of stomach gases for the sixth time. You are having a decidedly bad day. You need to act or you risk being sniffed out by your colleagues or your boss.

x32

Potential Dangers

SOLUTION: The busy man

1. Learn your lesson and forever avoid whatever you ate the previous evening.
2. Be patient. It will be a long day. Very, very long.
3. Grab a file folder and leave the office.
4. Walk the corridors of your office building with speed and determination to make it seem like you are incredibly busy. Avoid any interaction with your colleagues by saying, for example: "I really don't have time right now. We'll look at this tomorrow!"
5. Come back to your open-plan office and say things like: "Wow, what a crazy day. I haven't stopped the whole time!"
6. Go home as early as you can.

Expert opinion

If you let 12 farts out during breakfast, it doesn't take a genius to figure out you will have to deal with at least 250 more during your workday. Take sick leave and see a gastroenterologist immediately. If you don't have one, look one up at www.iwanttostopfartingnow.com.

Testimonial

I had many important conference calls planned for that day, so I took my phone and worked from the toilet. Between the smell I produced and the noise of other people in the toilet, it wasn't easy.

David, 55, client-services director

PROBLEM: You are being summoned, but you can't get up

OPEN-PLAN OFFICE

You are sitting at your desk, quietly suffering from the pain of holding in a fart onslaught that is boiling inside your intestines. A colleague asks if you could come with them for a minute to look at something. Standing up quickly would release your stomach gases immediately.

Potential Dangers

SOLUTION: The turtle

1. If it isn't far, stay on your chair and roll with it toward your colleague. Roll SLOWLY!
2. If you can't avoid getting up, firmly squeeze your buttocks without engaging your abdominal muscles.
3. Stand up much more SLOWLY than usual.
4. Walk slowly, taking VERY SMALL steps.
5. Come back slowly to your desk.
6. Sit down GENTLY.

Expert opinion

If your colleague makes a joke and you laugh, you're finished.

Testimonial

I moved slowly toward Sandra's desk. She dropped a pencil. I wanted to pick it up for her. You know the rest.

Silvio, 30, office-sales representative

PROBLEM: You sit down and your chair makes a farting noise

OPEN-PLAN
OFFICE

You sit down at your desk when your faux-leather chair makes a noise that sounds exactly like an actual fart. Several colleagues lift their heads and look at you suspiciously.

?

BRRRR!

Potential Dangers

SOLUTION: The commando

1. Don't try to demonstrate that it was the chair by attempting to reproduce the noise. You can never do it when you want to.
2. Simply accuse a colleague. Paul, for example.
3. Look at your colleague angrily and menacingly say something like this: "Paul, how many times do I have to remind you: you can't do this in an open-plan office!"
4. Paul will deny it, which is exactly what he needs to do for your colleagues to know it was him.

Expert opinion

I managed to find the right technique to sit on any chair with minimum noise, no matter the upholstery. I spent an entire weekend at IKEA and sat on over 80 chairs. There is only one – the leather POÄNG – that I haven't cracked yet. Contact me if you need a video demonstration for your chair.

Testimonial

My office chair made a particularly suspicious noise. I decided to recreate it 24 times per day for a whole week to show to my colleagues that it's the chair, not me. I thought this would give me good cover for an actual fart, too. It didn't. The noise I made was quite different – and louder – than the chair. My colleagues knew immediately.

Alexander, 42, head of marketing

The air conditioning breaks down. Life at your office continues as usual, and everyone continues to release their intestinal gases as always. The air soon smells putrid. It becomes difficult to continue working.

Potential Dangers

SOLUTION: DIY

1. Go toward the toilet and enter a cubicle.
2. Make pea-size paper balls.
3. Insert a paper ball into each nostril. Yes, you now have an effective home-made nasal air-purification filter. The paper balls should fill your nostrils, but not be visible to your colleagues.
4. Look in the mirror before exiting the toilet. If you resemble a hippopotamus, go back to step 2. Your paper balls are too big.
5. Go back to your desk but leave your office as soon as you can. Pretend, for example, that you must go to a meeting.

Expert opinion

Few people know that air conditioning doesn't only regulate temperature, but also captures odours. In offices with 100 employees, the air-conditioning filters usually measure 2 metres by 1 metre. The service personnel who change these filters every four years (as per the EU directive EuroF-2007-v1) are extremely well paid and can retire when they are just 45 years old.

Testimonial

I had to work on a Saturday and I ran into these maintenance people. The chaps looked like they came out of a Hollywood film about a chemical attack on a city: helmets with visors, gas masks, white airtight suits, double gloves…

Ben, 32, project manager

PROBLEM: Alone in your cubicle, you fart, but someone arrives at that moment

OPEN-PLAN
OFFICE

Your open-plan office is empty because all your colleagues are at a meeting. You seize this opportunity to relieve yourself quietly. As (bad) luck would have it, a colleague appears at that exact moment. She is walking towards you.

Potential Dangers

SOLUTION: Free food

1. Don't even try to dissipate the odour by waving your arms; you will only make the situation worse.
2. Act quickly. Tell your colleague that there are free croissants in the meeting room.
3. The temptation of free food is strong. Your colleague will turn immediately toward the meeting room.
4. In the future, think before you act and apply the PCR method scrupulously.

Expert opinion

It's unfathomable to think that you can still get caught in such a basic situation! If you are not using the PCR method *at all times*, there is nothing I can do for you.

Testimonial

I let out a big, fat, stinky fart. Greenflies started coming in through the open window and circled my chair like a dark, smelly cloud. My mentor walked in just as I was trying to chase them away with my keyboard.

David, 22, intern

PROBLEM: You fart at the end of the corridor, when someone arrives

HALLWAY

Alone in the corridor, you allow yourself to let one slip out. Bad luck: your boss appears at that moment and walks straight towards you. He will definitely pass through the contaminated zone.

Potential Dangers

SOLUTION: Caution

1. You need to act quickly.
2. Grimace and pinch your nose to show you are suffering from something.
3. Say: "Wow. It stinks in here!" Follow it up with: "Oh my God!"
4. When your boss is at your level, tell him: "Someone farted in the hallway. It's pretty bad... Good luck!"
5. Accuse a colleague. Paul, for example. "I bet it was Paul. He doesn't seem well today. He has spent most of the day in the toilet on the third floor."

Expert opinion

Let me remind you of two basic techniques when you need to release gas in a hallway:
1. If you pass by an office with the door wide open, fart there and leave quickly.
2. If this isn't possible, use the Fan Fish technique: use a folder to fan the air behind your *derriere* while continuing to walk ahead.

Testimonial

My boss told me: "I'm not an idiot, I know it was you."

Boris, 49, senior accountant

PROBLEM: You are walking towards the toilet and someone notices your peculiar behaviour

HALLWAY

You feel a strong internal pressure. You are walking towards the toilet gingerly to prevent the release of the troublesome gases. A colleague notices your strange demeanour and asks if everything is OK.

Potential Dangers

SOLUTION: The engagement

1. Tell your colleague: "I am participating in the World Slow-Down-for-the-Planet Day. I will be walking like a penguin all day to bring attention to the melting of the polar ice cap."
2. Ask your colleague if she wants to know more about it.
3. Afraid that you will end up asking her for money for your cause, too, she will leave rapidly. You will now be able to handle your problem in peace.
4. To avoid having to walk like a penguin all day, do what you need to do to avoid running into this colleague again for the rest of the day.

Expert opinion

If you work out your gluteal muscles efficiently, you will be able to walk quickly even when stomach gases are bothering you. Free tip: place this book between your buttocks and walk approximately a hundred metres without letting it fall. If a colleague asks to borrow the book afterward, say no.

Testimonial

I told a colleague I'm friendly with: "Leave me alone. If I speed up, it's coming out."

Vladimir, 53, quality engineer

PROBLEM: Your boss is walking behind you

HALLWAY

You are walking down a long hallway and have a strong urge to fart. But you notice that your boss is walking behind you. It is most certainly not the right time to let it go.

Potential Dangers

SOLUTION: The ideal son-in-law

1. Slow down progressively so that your boss catches up with you, then stop.
2. As your boss arrives at your level, press your back against the wall.
3. Smile and make a hand gesture inviting him to go before you.
4. Say: "After you. I wouldn't want to stop you; the whole company is counting on you."
5. Your boss, like all bosses, will appreciate your respect of hierarchy and will feel appreciated. He will think of you highly after this.
6. Once he is far away, release your fart in all serenity.

Expert opinion

Let me remind you that in order to make a great career in your company, it is of utmost importance that you walk quickly down the hallways, a folder under your arm or muttering in concern at your phone. This makes you look busy and important, even though in reality, you are not doing anything in particular.

Testimonial

My boss was coming up to me and I used this method. When he reached me, he said: "Ah, Steven, just the man I was looking for..." He went on and on for over 40 minutes about the importance of obtaining the ISO-30777BX certificate. Nobody in the company cares about that, least of all me. I don't even know what it is.

Steven, 37, automotive engineer

PROBLEM: You fart during the ride and someone enters

LIFT

You are alone in the lift and take advantage of this serene moment to let go of some inner gases. It smells bad. Suddenly, the lift slows down, the door opens, and someone walks in. You are in a tough spot.

Potential Dangers

SOLUTION: The poker face

1. When the door opens, calm your racing heart and start by identifying your companion to assess the gravity of the situation. Is it your boss, the entire board of directors, or just a colleague from another department?
2. Use your usual lift voice to say: "Hello." Nothing out of the ordinary here.
3. See which floor your lift-mate sets as their destination. It will determine the length of your agony.
4. Try to see out the corner of your eye if the other passenger is bothered by the smell.
5. If they seem to have noticed it, murmur upon exiting from the lift: "It stinks in this lift."
6. If not, leave the lift at your floor with a cheerful: "Bye!"

Expert opinion

Seriously, why would anyone think releasing warm methane in a space no bigger than $8m^3$ could possibly end well? Too many employees place way too much faith in their good luck when navigating their work space.

Testimonial

The door opened. My boss entered, then immediately stepped back and said: "In fact, I think I'll take the stairs. A little bit of exercise will do me good."

Julien, 41, logistics purchasing officer

PROBLEM: You enter the lift and the smell in it is horrific

You enter the lift in a hurry and press your floor. Just as the lift takes off, an unbearable smell envelops your nostrils.

Potential Dangers

SOLUTION: The escape game

1. Get over your gag reflex; you need to act quickly.
2. Don't attempt to hold your breath for the duration of the ride: holding your breath also holds the odour within your olfactory system, where it continues to affect you.
3. Check which floor you are on right now.
4. Press the button for the next floor.
5. If the smell is making it difficult for you to concentrate, press all buttons at the same time.
6. Approach the door and dash out as soon as it opens.
7. Take another lift to get to your destination.

Expert opinion

Every year, I visit the World Lift Association to meet the CEOs from the biggest lift manufacturers. I lobby for them to put stronger ventilation systems in their lifts. As the message of "optimal fart elimination" is very difficult to include in their marketing activities, they never do anything about it, and employees around the world continue to suffer.

Testimonial

The odour was untenable; I couldn't breathe. In panic, I pressed all the buttons. When the door opened, my boss was on the other side, waiting for the lift. He thought I was behaving like a three-year-old, having fun by pressing on all the lift buttons. Once the odour hit his nostrils, he must have also thought I farted. Not my best day at work...

Simon, 39, trader

PROBLEM: You enter the lift with several other people, and the smell is unbearable

There are a few of you waiting for the lift. When the door opens, you are too preoccupied with the lift etiquette and determining who should enter first to notice the horrific smell in the lift. As the door closes, you realise that you have entered a smelly trap.

Potential Dangers

SOLUTION: The lift rules

1. Apply the lift etiquette once more and show no emotion.
2. To do that, do what one usually does in a lift: read the plaque informing you of the maximum weight allowed, start mentally calculating the combined weight of everyone in the lift, analyse the shape of the buttons without forgetting the one with the little bell on it, look a bit in the mirror, observe the neon lights, notice the name of the lift manufacturer and the date of the next maintenance inspection... All of this with the empty lift expression.
3. Leave the lift as soon as the door opens and say nothing to all others who leave it as well, even though this is not their floor.
4. Next time, don't enter first to avoid being stuck at the back and, therefore, the last to leave the smelly box.

Expert opinion

I always let others enter before me. They think I'm excessively polite, but in fact, it's a technique that I have been using for over 10 years. I discreetly observe the faces of those who entered first. If a look of disgust starts spreading over their faces, I tell them I've decided to take the stairs instead.

Testimonial

I no longer enter the lift before others. If it stinks, I am blocked behind everybody else and I don't have access to the buttons to leave the lift at the nearest floor.

Sam, 51, head of production

PROBLEM: You need to break wind, but there are several others in the lift

There are several of you in the lift when you suddenly feel the urge to let go of your stomach gases. You do your best to hold it in, but the ride is too long. You won't make it.

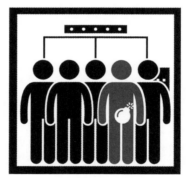

Potential Dangers

SOLUTION: The alignment of the planets

1. Approach the door without raising suspicion.
2. Turn around so that your back is against the door. You are going to attempt to evacuate your fart through it.
3. Place your buttocks so that your bum crack is aligned with the crack in the door. Find the right position by wiggling your bum imperceptibly.
4. Expel your gas, making sure the expression on your face is unchanged throughout.
5. The micro-current of air at the door crack will suck the fart to the outside. Don't let the propulsion be too speedy.

Expert opinion

How many times must I tell you? If you want to advance your career, you do not fart in the elevator!

Testimonial

I misjudged my flatulence. It was loud. The door was hollow inside, and my fart made it vibrate. A sound resembling a fog horn startled my fellow passengers.

Victor, 32, communication strategist

PROBLEM: The lift breaks down. You and your colleagues are stuck in it for three hours

You are in the lift with several of your colleagues when it breaks down and stops. In the ensuing silence, you press the button with the little bell to call for help. You are told someone will come to help you... in three hours at best.

Potential Dangers

SOLUTION: The precaution principle

1. Be brave: you will have to shatter a taboo.
2. Say these words exactly: "I'm very sorry to bring up the subject, but there are seven of us in this lift and the statistics don't lie. We will produce 7x5 flatulences in the next three hours. That's 35. This cabin is about to become a the equivalent of a nauseating hammam. We need to find a way to get some fresh air in here as quickly as possible."
3. Use all your strength to pull out the handrail from the lift wall.
4. Ram it into the ceiling to poke a hole in it.
5. Tell the others: "It's OK, we're safe. The methane can now be evacuated."
6. Wait patiently to be saved.

Expert opinion

Here's an insider tip for you. All the hotlines for lifts with the ISO29033 certificate follow the same procedure. Simply say this during your call: "There are many of us, and we all ate chili con carne for lunch today!" This will make them classify your situation as urgent and requiring immediate assistance. You will be rescued within 15 minutes instead of the usual 3 hours.

Testimonial

I work in maintenance for a lift company. We always work in pairs. With people that have been stuck for five hours or more, we draw straws to decide who will open the door and receive the "sirocco of death", which is the name for this situation in industry jargon.

Kevin, 28, lift repairman

PROBLEM: Your boss farts next to you

You are standing next to your boss in the lift. He farts.

Potential Dangers

SOLUTION: The long-awaited moment

1. Your boss knows what he has just done, which puts him in a weakened position.
2. Half of his brain is now dealing with this problem and you can use this unexpected psychological advantage to ask him for anything.
3. Say, for example:
   "I forgot to tell you, I'm going home at 2pm today."
   Or:
   "I won't finish my presentation by tonight like I promised."
   Or:
   "I won't be coming to the meeting tomorrow."
4. In the given situation, he should answer that he doesn't see a problem with that.
5. Leave with a cheerful "Goodbye!"

Expert opinion

You could also say nothing while the two of you are in the lift, and instead bring a signed and sealed letter to his mail slot. In the letter, write simply: "I know what you did in the lift." This will give you an upper hand for weeks to come.

Testimonial

When my boss farted, I had a laughing fit. The bastard fired me a week later.

Emily, 38, unemployed

PROBLEM: You are making noise in your stall

You are in your toilet stall. You fart, and it's a noisy one. There's no doubt that every other person in the toilets could hear you.

Potential Dangers

SOLUTION: The parrot technique

1. Don't use the typical methods (flushing the toilet, loud coughing, banging your feet around as if you were clumsy, etc.). They don't work.
2. You should prepare for such situations beforehand. Use your phone to occasionally tape a colleague having a phone conversation.
3. Play one of these recordings at full blast now. You want people in other stalls to think that it is the colleague whose voice they are hearing who farted. Be careful which recording you pick: if you use the voice of your boss, and he happens to be in the next stall, you'll be in trouble…
4. While the recording is playing, don't hold back. It will all be at the expense of your colleague.
5. Wait until everyone has left to come out.

Expert opinion

I am an amateur trumpetist in my spare time and I have a good understanding of air and sound flows. I've noticed that, by spreading my buttocks wide open with my hands when I sit down, I make a lot less noise. According to my measurements, it can be up to -7dB.

Testimonial

I worked on exhaust pipes for Formula 1. I used my knowledge to conceive a low-tech muffler that works marvellously. I am often asked for the assembly instructions. Here they are:

Several sheets of paper, finely rolled   Toilet-paper roll

Helmut, 49, engineer

67

PROBLEM: The person in the neighbouring stall is relieving himself loudly, which makes you freeze

You are in one of the stalls in the office toilet, ready to relieve some gas. Someone is in the stall next to yours, farting without reservation. It's incredibly loud and frequent. It makes you freeze completely. You are blocked and can't seem to be able to relieve yourself.

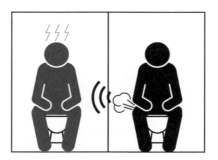

Potential Dangers

SOLUTION: A voyage through space and time

1. Cover your ears with your hands.
2. Breathe slowly. (Not through the nose!)
3. Relax by imagining yourself somewhere safe and comfortable: your own bathroom at home.
4. Visualise the tiles, the IKEA lamp on the ceiling, the basket of magazines for toilet reading...
5. Mentally pick up one of your celebrity magazines and start leafing through it.
6. You should now be sufficiently relaxed to relieve yourself and fart.

Expert opinion

If this is often a problem for you, train at home. Go to the toilet and ask your partner or roommate to sit on the other side of the door, playing YouTube videos with farting sounds.

Testimonial

I am the guy from the testimonial on page 67. You should know that my muffler works as a noise reduction device for the ears as well. Don't use the one created previously; I suggest you keep two of them handy.

Helmut, still 49, still engineer

PROBLEM: You are making noise, and someone calls you from outside

You are relieving yourself noisily in one of the toilet stalls. Unfortunately, someone hears you from outside. Worse yet, this colleague knocks on the door and asks: "Everything all right in there?"

Potential Dangers

SOLUTION: The royal missive

1. Don't answer: "Yes, yes, everything is fine. I'm almost done!" Your colleague will immediately recognize you.
2. Take a piece of toilet paper and write on it: "Everything is fine, I just have diarrhoea. I often do."
3. Sign it with the name of a colleague you dislike. Paul, for example.
4. Before you leave the stall, wait until the path is clear.

Expert opinion

Whenever I hear tell-tale noises in one of the stalls and I know that someone I don't like is in there, I like to knock on their door to ask if everything is OK. I know that this makes them uncomfortable and they are then afraid to leave until I have left the toilet.

Testimonial

Not knowing exactly what to do, I didn't answer — not even the third time my colleague asked if everything was OK. This made him worry that someone had fainted in the stall, so he left to look for help. He came back with my boss and two other colleagues. They tore down the door by ramming the mail cart into it. They found me inside with my trousers around my ankles, reading news on my smartphone...

Martin, 42, order handler

PROBLEM: You are using the urinal next to a colleague, and you accidentally let one rip

You are standing facing the urinal. You are feeling relaxed and you let out a fart by accident. A colleague is standing near to you. It's awkward.

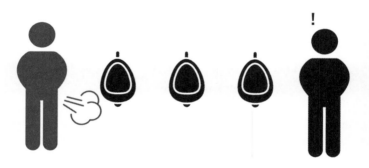

Potential Dangers

SOLUTION: Keep a lid on it

1. You should continue as if nothing had happened. This is one of the unwritten rules of urinals in company toilets.
2. By no means should you look at your colleague, because his reproachful eyes could make you unable to pee. Continue to stare at the wall emptily.
3. In this situation, you should never say things like:
   "You should leave. In about ten seconds, it will smell really bad around here."
   Or:
   "Oops, I didn't see that one coming!"
4. Shake it off, flush, wash your hands, and leave the toilet.

Expert opinion

Let me remind you that the urinals are governed by rules that have never been written down, but that hold just the same: you should always use the urinal that is the furthest away from another person. If there are multiple users, you should always keep a courtesy urinal between each of you.

Testimonial

We were six in line, each with his own urinal. As I was leaving, I let a silent one go. I noticed that my colleagues were either pinching their noses or grimacing. They didn't seem to be enjoying this short moment of relaxation at work.

Thomas, 31, engineer

PROBLEM: You leave the toilet and your clothes smell very bad

You went to the toilet to fart, but you stayed in there a tad too long. Your clothes are infused with the smell that you just released. When you leave your stall, you are like a stinky dungball rolling along.

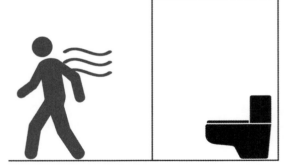

Potential Dangers

SOLUTION: Freshening up

1. Don't try to fix the situation by spraying your clothes with air freshener. You will smell of "Lotus of Sichuan" all day, and besides, your colleagues will recognize immediately the familiar scent and figure you out.
2. Lock the main toilet door.
3. Take off your trousers, your shirt and your pullover or blazer.
4. Use one of the sinks to wash your clothes by hand with hand soap.
5. Wring out your clothes by twisting them strongly.
6. Use the hand dryer to dry your clothes. It will take you around 2–3 hours for your whole outfit.

Expert opinion

Don't try to rub your clothes with the toilet-bowl cleaning product hanging in the toilet. They tend to have bleach in them and will stain your clothes irreparably.

Testimonial

I forgot to lock the door and my boss walked in on me while I was doing my laundry. I was face to face with him in only my underpants. I didn't have the courage to explain what I was doing.

Maxime, 34, management accountant

PROBLEM: You stink up a stall and leave just as a colleague enters

You have just farted in the office toilet, and the smell is monstrous. As you are exiting, you run into a colleague who is clearly on his way to the toilet.

Potential Dangers

SOLUTION: The blame game

1. Keep walking toward your colleague.
2. With an expression of utter shock, tell him that someone let out a stinker in the toilet.
3. Use denial or questioning to confirm that you are not the source of the smell. Say, for example: "I wonder who was in there that could…"
4. If possible, blame someone else who could be a plausible culprit. Say, for example: "I think it was Paul; he was just leaving as I came in."
5. If the odour is particularly unbearable, make sure you say that you weren't able to even go in yourself because of the smell.

Expert opinion

This is a method that requires some cold-bloodedness. Accuse the poor soul you usually blame: Paul. If this Paul is already famous in your company, enjoy yourself and have fun farting in the toilet!

Testimonial

I felt horrible — the odour was dreadful. I'm shy by nature and I really feared what my colleague might think, or even say, especially since he is known for not holding back his opinions. Just before leaving the restroom, I thought of Michael from accounting, who had just been bragging that morning about a boozy night out. I think that's what saved me…

Ben, 43, billing services

PROBLEM: You let out a noisy one during an important meeting

You are in a meeting with your team and your boss. Expecting a quiet one, you fart. Bad call: a sound leaving nothing to the imagination awakens your dozing colleagues.

Potential Dangers

SOLUTION: The mirror technique

1. To avoid being identified, you will need to behave just like everyone else around the table: act surprised and look left and right as if you are trying to identify the source of this suspicious sound.
2. Careful: this technique isn't as easy as it seems. It often happens that the guilty party reacts with three seconds of delay, which is enough to give them away.
3. You need to be mentally prepared to act surprised before you fart so that you can react like any other employee surprised by someone farting, without overdoing it. Being among the first to look around is key. According to our studies – for which we used high-speed cameras at 1000 images/second – it all hangs on one tenth of a second.
4. After a few moments of futile search, go back to the meeting.

Expert opinion

Knowing how to feign surprise will be very useful in many situations when you fart in a group of people. Train at home:
1. Find your fart-onomatopoeia (i.e. "Ugh!" "Yuck!" "Phew!")
2. Practise the appropriate facial expressions and the right speech volume in front of your bathroom mirror.

Testimonial

When I practise at home, I use Mr Hayatt's technique. As soon as my husband shouts the word "Fart!" I have to put on my surprised face and look for the culprit. The shout can come at any moment, just like a fart. My husband thinks I'm progressing fast.

Angelina, 38, socio-cultural animator

PROBLEM: You let out a smelly one during an important meeting

MEETING ROOM

You are in a meeting with your boss and your colleagues. Thinking you can make a silent and odourless one, you let one go. Silent it was. Odourless it was not.

Potential Dangers

SOLUTION: The repositioning

1. Pick the shyest participant of the meeting. Nicholas, for example.
2. Raise your hand and say: "I'm very sorry to interrupt this meeting, but Nicholas just farted, and the smell is unbearable in this part of the room."
3. Stand up and march toward the door.
4. Open the door and start swinging it back and forth to try to ventilate the meeting room.
5. Close the door and sit on another chair; one that is the furthest away from Nicholas.
6. Ask your colleagues for your things.

Expert opinion

I never do meetings that last longer than 40 minutes. Everyone thinks it's because I'm so efficient, but it's actually because this is the longest I can go without farting.

Testimonial

The smell I emitted was particularly awful, so I decided to use this method. My colleagues followed my example and they all also moved away from the colleague I accused, who ended up sitting completely alone. He was so embarrassed that he left the meeting 10 minutes later.

Mark, 30, legal advisor

PROBLEM: You are in the middle of a presentation

You are making a presentation in front of your boss and your colleagues. Public speaking stresses you and you can't control yourself. You fart loudly.

Potential Dangers

SOLUTION: Out of the box

1. If your audience was drowsy, you certainly have their attention now...
2. Say: "I just farted, yes! Can anybody tell me why?"
3. Nobody will have the answer to that.
4. Tell them exactly the following: "I farted to show you what is missing in this company. As soon as someone innovates, you stigmatize them for thinking out of the box. And yet, if we want our company to stay agile, visionary, and capable of seizing the opportunities that this changing world is giving us, we need to forget convention and take the road less travelled!"
5. Conclude by saying: "We will come back to this. Let's go to the next slide."

Expert opinion

I would like to take this opportunity to congratulate the readers of this book for doing exactly that – thinking outside of the box by reading this book, rather than Malcolm Gladwell's *Outliers: The Story of Success* or some other business book that everybody is reading.

Testimonial

I was competing with a colleague for a promotion. He was giving an important presentation. An hour before it was set to begin, I uploaded mega_fart.mp3 on his smartphone, and set it as the notification sound for all his incoming calls and messages. A week later I got promoted, not him.

Clara, 27, head of human resources

PROBLEM: Someone farts and everyone looks at you

MEETING ROOM

You are participating in a meeting with your colleagues and your boss. For once, you are actually enjoying the meeting, but someone suddenly lets one rip very loudly and everyone looks at you. It wasn't you!

Potential Dangers

SOLUTION: The counter-attack

1. Don't say: "But it wasn't me!" This is the excuse of the guilty, and your colleagues know this.
2. Identify the true culprit. Tip: it's the one who is avoiding eye contact with you. Paul, for example.
3. Look at him sternly and say: "Paul, everyone thinks it's me. Please tell us the truth. Everyone will forgive you."
4. Follow up by suggesting a five-minute break, so that the odour can dissipate. Tell your colleagues that Paul is buying everyone a cup of coffee.

Expert opinion

If people often look at you in such situations, ask yourself why and improve your behaviour at work. It is entirely possible that your colleagues are calling you Mr Fart behind your back.

Testimonial

I know that it doesn't concern this situation, but I don't know where else to ask this question. When someone touches my arm, I fart. Is this normal? What can I do?

Pablo, 45, purchasing manager

PROBLEM: You let out a stinker and people leave in outrage

MEETING ROOM

You farted, and it's an incredibly smelly one. Some of your colleagues leave in outrage, heaving.

Potential Dangers

SOLUTION: The mass effect

1. When your colleagues get up to leave, stand up as well and start putting away your things noisily.
2. When you reach the door, say to no one in particular: "I don't know which one of you did this, but it's really not OK because this meeting was incredibly interesting and important for our company."
3. Continue fuming in the hallway: "How do you expect this company to make any money with imbeciles like yourselves?"

Expert opinion

When I am in meetings that are useless and don't seem like they will ever end, I tend to leave the room while accusing the meeting organizer of flatulence.

Testimonial

I treated myself to an extra-large kebab, with extra onions. The result was extra-large. Everyone left the meeting – there was only me left. After a minute or so, I had to leave as well.

Raoul, 47, creative director

PROBLEM: You stuffed your face during a company breakfast and you feel bloated

The organizer of the morning meeting kindly brought a plate of croissants and fruit for everyone. You love food, especially when it's free, so you stuffed yourself. Thirty minutes later, you are horribly bloated and facing a series of farts.

Potential Dangers

SOLUTION: The new lotus position

1. Stop eating (11 croissants, 3 bananas and 2 peaches should be enough)!
2. Sit up, with your back straight.
3. Clench your gluteal muscles as much as you can.
4. You will prevent any accidents by placing your hands discreetly under your chair and pulling the chair upwards to press your buttocks into the seat of your chair (do as if you were going to lift the chair with you in it).
5. Stay in this position until the end of the meeting. Try looking relaxed, despite the effort.
6. As soon as the last meeting participant has left, release your hold, and the accumulated gas.

Expert opinion

Meetings with food are three times less productive than any others. The employees are using 70% of their brain to contemplate dilemmas such as:

• Should I have the fourth croissant, or would that be too much?
• Paul had four, she had two, the boss had four... Could I have a fifth one?
• This one probably has the vanilla filling.
• Shit, this one isn't good... How can I get rid of this crappy almond viennoiserie?

Testimonial

I told myself it would be better to leave the conference room. I got up gingerly. As luck would have it, my phone fell out of my pocket. I bent to retrieve it, and this released the fart exactly in the wrong direction and at the wrong height.

Christian, 47, waiting to be transferred abroad

PROBLEM: You let out a stinker next to the photocopier just as a colleague arrives

You considerately retreated to the copy room to relieve yourself. In a stroke of bad luck, a colleague enters the room at that same moment.

Potential Dangers

SOLUTION: Bomb scare

1. As soon as you notice your colleague, signal to him to stop where he is.
2. Tell him not to enter because it's hell in there. Let him know that Paul was there just before you and apparently farted multiple times.
3. Tell him to come back in 20 minutes when it will be possible to breathe again.

Expert opinion

With digital transformation, office workers are printing and copying much less, and copy rooms are becoming a thing of the past. Sadly, we are thus losing one of the safest and most convenient places for farting discreetly at work.

Testimonial

I tried to prevent my colleague from approaching by telling him that the machine broke down. He said he would try to repair it. He bent into the cloud of odour and jumped up immediately: "Wow. I'll come back later. I'm going to... ummm, find a screwdriver." He practically ran out.

Olivia, 30, product range manager

PROBLEM: Your office stinks

YOUR OWN OFFICE

You have taken to relieving yourself in the privacy of your own office. Bad idea: a foul smell spreads all over the office and seems to stay.

Potential Dangers

SOLUTION: The cat sand

1. Based on our experience, the smells that are the most difficult to remove are in the carpet. You will have to capture your own odours.
2. Measure your office floor's surface area and multiply it by 10cm to calculate its volume. Go to a pet store and buy the appropriate amount of cat litter.
3. On a Friday evening when everyone has gone home, spread the cat litter across the office floor, 10cm thick.
4. Leave it there for a weekend. Come back early on Monday morning to remove the cat litter and return your office to normal.
5. On another weekend, come to the office and give it a fresh coat of paint.

Expert opinion

I was contacted by an employee who had this problem in his office. He asked me to meet him there. I couldn't stay longer than two minutes.

Testimonial

I used this technique and the odour disappeared. It all went well until after the weekend when I came to remove the cat litter. My boss came to the office unannounced and caught me in the act. He saw me just when I was leaving with the wheelbarrow I'd borrowed at a nearby construction site.

Christine, 29, financial analyst

PROBLEM: You break wind just as someone enters your office

YOUR OWN OFFICE

You allow yourself to break wind and a horrendous smell floods your office. A colleague enters without knocking to discuss an urgent matter.

Potential Dangers

SOLUTION: The strength is in unity

1. Don't panic. This is your office: you have at least some control of the situation.
2. Tell your colleague: "Don't enter, the boss was just here, and she farted horribly. It was ten minutes ago and it still stinks!"
3. Ask them for help.
4. Give your colleague a file folder and take one yourself.
5. Use the folders as fans and ventilate the room.
6. Thank them profusely.

Expert opinion

For those who don't use the PCR technique, know that letting a colleague enter in the hope that he won't notice your one-gun salute is extremely dangerous. It rarely works – never, in fact!

Testimonial

My colleague entered without knocking. She stopped mid-sentence and said: "Ehm, actually, never mind, it's not important. I'll come back later."

William, 52, head of accounting

PROBLEM: You simply must fart, but your boss won't leave your office

YOUR OWN OFFICE

Your boss has been in your office for a while now. The urge to fart is becoming unbearable. The problem: your boss isn't showing any signs of wanting to leave.

Potential Dangers

SOLUTION: The 30% method

1. Use the 30% raise technique, which has also proven to be effective in situations when you need to poo (see our book *How to Poo at Work*).
2. To do this, interrupt your boss and say: "This reminds me, we were going to meet to discuss my promotion and my raise. We said 30%, right?"
3. Your boss will suddenly remember he has somewhere to be right at that minute.
4. Watch him leave. You are now free to relieve yourself.
5. Open the window immediately. He might return for a pen, folder or phone that he accidentally left behind in his haste.

Expert opinion

Even if you are sure you could do a silent one, never do it with your boss present. Remember your luck: in reality, it's usually both loud and smelly.

Testimonial

We had been behind the closed doors of my office for five hours, working on a complicated project. I sneezed, and it all come out at once.

Patrick, 37, zone manager

PROBLEM: Your colleague breaks wind in your office

YOUR OWN OFFICE

You are having a conversation with a colleague in your office. He forgets his manners and the rules of peaceful coexistence, and lets one rip. In your office!

Potential Dangers

SOLUTION: Compassion

1. Your colleague is worried. He hopes you will not smell it.
2. Look him in the eyes for two seconds without saying anything. He will understand that you know what he did.
3. Suggest you grab a cup of coffee outside.
4. Let him pay. He knows why.

Expert opinion

People who let themselves fart in other people's offices annoy me. I have been telling them for the past two years: "Farting in a colleague's office is just like farting in their home, on their pillow."

Testimonial

My colleague said: "Sorry. I farted."
"I know," I replied.

Emma, 26, product manager

PROBLEM: You are alone in your office and you fart. The smell becomes unbearable

YOUR OWN OFFICE

You are in your own office and you relieve yourself of some stomach gas. A few moments later, the odour starts to bother you. It is quite awful.

Potential Dangers

SOLUTION: Coffee break

1. Don't open the window. If a colleague were to enter your office right then, there would be little need to guess what had happened, what with the window open and the remaining odour lingering in the air.
2. Hold your breath and try to air out the room using a file folder as a fan. Careful: don't use this technique if you have an office with glass walls. A colleague or your boss could figure out what happened from your grimace and your fanning.
3. You should probably simply take a coffee break.
4. According to our tests, it takes four minutes with air conditioning set to medium to evacuate strong odours from an office. Take your time in the break room and use it for networking.

Expert opinion

The level of odour perception varies from person to person. We get used to bad odours we produce ourselves, but not to those of others. If your own smell bothers you, just imagine what it must be like for everyone else.

Testimonial

I did go to grab a coffee, but this particular flatulence was tenacious. It followed me to the coffee machine.

Justin, 29, customer relations

PROBLEM: You are spraying air freshener when your boss enters

YOUR OWN OFFICE

You are in your office when you break wind. The smell is such that it cannot go unnoticed. You decide to spray the office with "Lemon Cinnamon" air freshener. Right then, your boss enters and catches you in the act.

Potential Dangers

SOLUTION: The neo-productivity

1. Don't panic: you *can* get out of this one. Yes, really!
2. Tell your boss that he came at just the right moment because you have just returned from a workshop "Productivity and Wellness at Work". Tell him that your coach suggested you perfume your office to give your creativity a boost.
3. As your boss looks at you suspiciously, add: "I love my job, and I'm ready to give my all to this company! And on top of it, I have a great boss!"
4. This will stoke his ego and he will forget the strange smell in your office.
5. Calmly answer the question he came to ask you and go back to work with a smile on your face.

Expert opinion

When you buy an air deodoriser, try not to be a victim of marketing. Don't be tempted by exotic perfumes, and opt instead for professional equipment that works. These products are perfume-free and really catch odour. I created a professional line of air deodorisers. Contact me.

Testimonial

My boss caught me with the air freshener in my hand. I told him I had to work with Eddie, the colleague who is known throughout the company for his bad body odour. My boss said: "Good idea, Juliet. I have a meeting with Eddie in ten minutes in my office. Can I borrow your spray?"

Juliet, 31, office manager

PROBLEM: You let rip such a noisy one that people in the hallway can hear you

YOUR OWN OFFICE

You are alone in your office, and you let one go. The forceful sound you emit confirms that it was high time you did it. The problem: the office walls are so thin that your fart could be heard down the hallway.

Potential Dangers

SOLUTION: Fragmentation bomb

1. You will simulate a lively exchange in your office with a colleague you dislike. Paul, for example.
2. Say loudly: "Paul, can you please explain why you farted in MY office and not your own?"
3. Pause and then say even louder: "Come on, it will stink for at least ten minutes in here now!"
4. Open the window and continue grumbling so that your colleagues understand that the odour Paul produced is truly horrendous.
5. No, Paul is not *actually* in your office.

Expert opinion

I sound-proofed my office with Kevlar plaques filled with steel wool. I get them from the factory that sound-proofs control towers of US airports. It works, I can tell you that!

Testimonial

I take this subject very seriously. So seriously that I made sure I knew what I could really do in my office without being heard outside. One weekend, I brought my wife and my in-laws with me to the office. We spent two hours simulating all kinds of fart sounds and checking which could be heard on the other side of the partition.

Arthur, 45, architect

PROBLEM: The office cafeteria goes vegan

CAFETERIA

Your company has embraced environmentally friendly, well-being philosophy. Everyone receives an e-mail informing you that meals such as steak and fries will disappear from the menu to be replaced by a new, entirely vegan, fibre-rich offering. The limits of everyone's intestines are about to get tested, as is your office building's air-conditioning system.

Potential Dangers

SOLUTION: Adapting to the transition

1. You need to quickly learn to pick your cafeteria meals carefully or your intestines – and then nostrils – will suffer.
2. IMPORTANT: Avoid the combination of cabbage + beans + prunes.
3. Give priority to the safety of your transition over satiety: start with small quantities and increase them slowly.
4. Take time to chew. As the saying goes: "Food well chewed, sphincter secured."
5. Your intestines will need around three months to adapt and go back to the usual 8–15 farts per day.
6. If during the adaptation period you find you miss meat immensely, look at pictures of ham slices during boring meetings.

Expert opinion

If you are the boss and you are thinking of turning your office cafeteria vegan, know that you should add new items in your investment spending: extra toilet paper and an upgraded ventilation system.

Testimonial

Three days after going vegan, everybody at the company was having all sorts of problems. There were green flies everywhere in the building. Our human resources department tackled the problem by giving each employee a fly swatter in company colours embossed with the slogan: "Be vegan, be happy!"

Nina, 42, receptionist

PROBLEM: The moment you stink up the smoking room, your boss arrives for a smoke

You come to fart in the smoking room, taking advantage of its excellent ventilation system. The problem: your boss enters and walks into an atrocious smell.

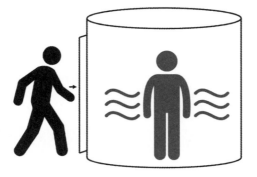

Potential Dangers

SOLUTION: The new flavour

1. Even though you feel trapped in this glass box, admit nothing; you can still come out of this safely.
2. Warn your boss that there is a strange smell in the smoking room today.
3. Explain that one of your colleagues – Paul, for example – came in to try out one of the new flavours of electronic cigarettes that he secretly creates at home. Tell your boss that Paul plans to open his own company and quit his job.
4. Add: "He says the perfume is called 'Alaska Spruce'. Actually, I think it smells like the toilet on the second floor at the end of the week."
5. Change the subject and leave the smoking room soon under the pretext that you have an important project to finish.

Expert opinion

Farting at work has only become problematic since smoking at work was banned. In the 1960s, everyone could fart freely and risk nothing as the tobacco smell covered up everything. The yellowing of walls and curtains was not only due to the cigarette smoke.

Testimonial

My boss joined me in the smoking room. We looked at each other. We both knew that the other one didn't smoke. We therefore knew exactly what both of us had come to do in the smoking room.

Albert, 50, department manager

PROBLEM: You are outside with a group of colleagues and you let one rip

COMPANY COURTYARD

You don't feel like working, so you join your smoking colleagues for the fourth coffee this morning. You are with them in front of the building, in the courtyard or the space where smoking is allowed. You fart. It stinks.

Potential Dangers

SOLUTION: Dispersion

1. Think of a person that nobody in the company likes. Paul, for example.
2. Tell your colleagues that they need to leave quickly because you saw Paul coming out, and he will probably want to talk to you again about his project of obtaining the new ISO Quality standard and the convergence 2028 project.
3. Mention also that he is in the company of Nadine, who is again collecting donations for orphans in Bulgaria.
4. Follow your leaving colleagues and go back to work.
5. Send an e-mail, then invite some other colleagues for a well-deserved coffee break.

Expert opinion

If you position yourself in a way that you are facing your colleagues and facing the wind, the coffee/smoke break outside is one of the three best places to relieve yourself of gas safely. The space is ventilated, non-confined, a bit noisy, and the cigarette smoke has a strong enough smell to cover any bodily gases you emit.

Testimonial

I didn't notice that an ashtray was right behind my back. I farted and emptied half of it.

Sofia, 41, book editor

PROBLEM: You fart loudly in your boss's office

BOSS'S OFFICE

You thought you could release your stomach gas without making a sound. You do make a sound. Your boss doesn't say anything, but his eyes show clearly that he heard you. You won't score points with him on this one.

Potential Dangers

SOLUTION: The professional conscience

1. You were stupid enough to fart in your boss's office! You have no other option but to break one of the golden rules of farting at work: apologize.
2. Lie to your boss that you have been ill for over a week, and that your doctor told you to stay home, but that you simply couldn't bring yourself to let him and the team down.
3. Listen to the corporate-speak that your boss will surely impart on you: "Please know that I appreciate your drive, but don't put your health and the health of others at risk."
4. Go back to what you were doing before. He has probably already forgotten what you just told him and is thinking about his next meeting, for which he is already very late.

Expert opinion

According to my estimates, admitting to one flatulency is the equivalent of two years of sucking up to your boss. Extra hours, feigning interest during meetings, e-mails sent at 6 a.m. during your holidays, heartfelt messages on his birthday – all for naught.

Testimonial

I farted, and my boss started laughing. I laughed nervously as well. He thought I found the subject funny as well. He has been sending me fart videos each morning ever since, and then came to my cubicle to ask me loudly: "So, Stephen, what did you think of that video of the farting panda? Epic, right?" and "Did you see the one with the kitten that blows out the candles?"

Stephen, 30, robotics engineer

PROBLEM: You let out a stinker in your boss's office

BOSS'S OFFICE

You sneakily fart in your boss's office. You are secretly congratulating yourself for having done a quiet one. Three seconds later, you mournfully realize it was a very smelly one.

Potential Dangers

SOLUTION: The filtering punishment

1. Create a mental image of the cloud of pollution you have just produced.
2. Try to inhale the cloud in its entirety through your mouth.
3. Hold your breath as long as possible to give your lungs time to filter the tainted air you inhaled.
4. Feign accidentally dropping something on the floor. While bending, exhale behind you.
5. Never blow air in the direction of your boss. Your lungs probably couldn't filter out the whole fart.
6. Have a mint.

Expert opinion

Here's a piece of advice that I never thought I would have to spell out: never let out your first flatulence of the day in your boss's office. You haven't yet established if your farts are revolting as you are having a "stinky day".

Testimonial

When the odour hit my boss's nostrils, she didn't say anything. Instead, she got up to open the window and stayed there for the remainder of our meeting. She gave me 15 new dossiers to deal with. Her cold eyes were saying: "You know exactly why I'm giving you these. You should never have done this in my office!"

Lea, 38, media planner

PROBLEM: Your boss is an incorrigible farter; you don't want to go to his office anymore

BOSS'S OFFICE

Your superior farts in his office constantly. His office always smells foul. He is so used to his odour that he doesn't realize you and your colleagues suffer when he asks you to see him in his office. Your colleagues are doing everything to avoid going there.

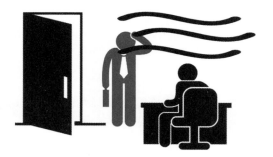

Potential Dangers

SOLUTION: Continuous improvements

1. If you don't want to suffer anymore, you will need to try to improve the air quality in his office.
2. Go and see the maintenance supervisor. Explain your problem and ask him to double the strength of ventilation in your boss's office.
3. Go to the supermarket, specifically the car accessories aisle, and buy a seat deodorant. When your boss isn't there, empty the entire spray can into his chair, as well as any carpets.
4. In the "Toiletries and Exoticism" section, buy disinfecting toilet tablets with "Polar Fresh" scent to stick under his table and behind the ventilation cover.*
5. Have a large exotic plant delivered to his office for his birthday. It will transform hot and humid air into fresh, oxygen-rich air.

*If the ventilation is on the ceiling, ask another long-suffering colleague to give you a leg up.

Expert opinion

University courses in human resources never broach the subject of excessive flatulence at work. And yet, directors of human resources are constantly reaching out to me when faced with high-potential individuals whose offices smell... bad. The three of us then sit down together to discuss it. I always begin our sessions by saying: "I won't beat around the bush, Mr X. You are known as Mr Fart in this company. I understand your surprise, but don't worry. Together, we can turn this into a great opportunity for your career."

Testimonial

The good news: my farting boss was fired. Bad news: I got his office.

Igor, 48, head of after-sales service

PROBLEM: You share a hotel room with a colleague

HOTEL

You are away on a team-building retreat and you share a room with a colleague. You find yourself in a tiny room with the toilet behind a thin partition that doesn't block any sound. You need to go in there to fart.

Potential Dangers

SOLUTION: A moment of well-being

1. Even though we usually advise against this technique, you won't have any choice but to create new noises to cover up your farts.
2. Open the water tap in the bathroom sink and let the water run in the shower simultaneously. Use very hot water to create vapour, which will hopefully trigger the ventilation.
3. Turn on the hair dryer.
4. Fart.
5. Once finished, empty all the complimentary shower-gel, shampoo and body-lotion bottles into the toilet. Use the toilet brush to swirl it vigorously. This should perfume the room and cover up your gas odour.
6. Undress, wet your face, and leave the bathroom in a bathrobe, as if you had just taken a nice shower.

Expert opinion

I beg you, stop killing your careers so stupidly! How does farting right next to your colleague or boss seem better than going to the toilet in the lobby or even just outside?

Testimonial

My colleague had farted in the bathroom. I went in to take a shower. I came out immediately and told him I had decided to shower after breakfast.

Mathias, 39, country manager

PROBLEM: You are in the car with your boss and you release a smelly fart

COMPANY CAR

You take advantage of the noise of the accelerating car to cover up the sound of your fart. The horror: you let out a smelly one. Your boss knows that he hasn't farted recently. It could have only been you.

Potential Dangers

SOLUTION: Wisdom

1. You committed an error, and you will have to face the consequences.
2. Don't say: "I'm sorry, I didn't think it would smell."
3. Neither should you open the window; this would equal admission.
4. Your boss will not say anything. You will have to be patient and sit through the time it takes for the odour to dissipate.
5. You can discreetly touch the air conditioning to try to speed up this process. Don't turn it all the way up: that would be the same as admitting you did it.
6. Your boss will be concentrating on the fact that you have made an error, and he is mad at you. Try to distract him by turning on the radio or by talking about the weather.

Expert opinion

Don't try to quietly open the door while the car is stopped; the warning system will beep like mad.

Testimonial

After three minutes, the odour was just as strong. My boss stopped on the hard shoulder. Without uttering a single word, he got out of the car and opened all the doors, starting with mine. We left five minutes later. The rest of the trip was very, very long.

Leopold, 28, business developer

PROBLEM: You are in the car with your boss and he farts

COMPANY CAR

You are in the car with your boss. He suddenly goes quiet. He farted. It smells very bad.

Potential Dangers

SOLUTION: The glory day

1. Your boss is ill at ease and stays quiet. Take advantage of this situation to take your revenge.
2. He is wondering if you could smell it. Show him that you did, but don't say anything.
3. Start by turning the ventilation up.
4. Crack open the window. One symbolic centimetre is enough.
5. Pick up a file folder and make slow fanning movements.
6. Blow softly and discreetly in his direction, as if you are trying to send the smell back toward him.

Expert opinion

I know a sadistic CEO who took sick pleasure in turning on the air-recycling button after farting. I still don't understand how he was able to manage his company and lead his teams.

Testimonial

There were only the two of us in the car. My boss farted and the bastard accused me of doing it!

Alicia, 34, key account manager

PROBLEM: You are in the first row at a lecture and you interrupt the CEO by farting

AMPHITHEATRE

You are sitting in the first row, listening to a speech by the CEO. Suddenly, you fart much louder than you anticipated. The CEO stops mid-sentence and looks at you sternly.

Potential Dangers

SOLUTION: Guilt transfer

1. Show no sign of guilt.
2. Signal to your CEO with a complicit look that something unusual has, indeed, just happened.
3. Bravely hold his stare and point your finger at the person sitting next to you, to indicate it came from them.
4. Stand up holding your nose and find a seat at least three rows further down.

Expert opinion

This reminds me: I will never understand why so many people would give their left buttock to be at one of Apple's keynotes. I did the maths. 2000 journalists x 3 hours x 1 flatulency/hour/person = 6000 farts in an enclosed space! Why would one want to inflict such a thing upon oneself just to find out that the iPhone Wx+ is coming out in two new colours?

Testimonial

I broke a silent but stinky one, and the odour went directly toward the big boss at the podium. After some hand ventilation, he understood that it wouldn't go away. He said something about the air conditioning being too strong where he was standing as a pretext to move the podium 10 metres to the right.

Zoe, 44, brand manager

PROBLEM: You fart and the microphone picks it up

AMPHITHEATRE

You are waiting for your turn to speak at a conference. You put the microphone down next to you on the couch and forget it's on. You fart. The sound is amplified throughout the amphitheatre.

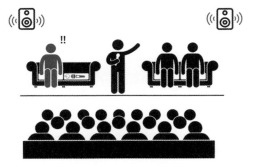

Potential Dangers

SOLUTION: Actor's studio

1. Don't use the microphone to apologize to the audience. At this moment, it is not possible to identify the source of the detonating sound. You should, therefore, react just like all the other people in the room.
2. To do this, look surprised, then burst out laughing, then look around to find the one who did it, still smiling.
3. When you take the stage, hint at the real culprit: "Thank you, Mr Paul, for this explosive speech, full of fertile ideas for a strong wind of change that will propel us all to success."

Expert opinion

If you are waiting for your turn to speak and wearing a tie-clip microphone, remember also not to burp by discreetly lowering your head.

Testimonial

I reacted with lightning speed. I grabbed my microphone and did beatbox for a good minute before letting my boss continue his speech.

Tony, 28, legal assistant

PROBLEM: You stand up to ask a question, with dire consequences

AMPHITHEATRE

Dead silence reigns in the amphitheatre after your CEO's intervention. You want to make a good impression and break the silence. You stand up to ask a question, even though you feel a strong urge to fart. As you get up to grab the microphone from the host, you accidentally let out a loud dose of flatulence that you have been holding in for the past 20 minutes. Two hundred people in the hall hear you because the sound is picked up by the microphone.

Potential Dangers

SOLUTION: A new life

1. Go out and head straight home. Don't come back to the office, ever. (It is futile to attempt to build a career in this company. It's over.)
2. Update your CV.
3. Update your LinkedIn profile.
4. Subscribe to newsletters at job sites.
5. Apply for jobs that match your profile.
6. Don't ask for a recommendation letter.

Expert opinion

I can confirm that it is, indeed, impossible to build a career in the company where everyone calls you Mr Fart or variations thereof.

Testimonial

I didn't even get a chance to ask my question. The CEO interrupted me and demolished me in front of everyone by saying: "Thank you, Thomas. Now, does anyone have another question?"

Thomas, 37, ex-partnerships manager

CHAPTER 4: FARTING YOUR WAY TO THE TOP

> *"If you want to ensure career advancement, get better at farting at work and use it against your boss."*
> Tom Hayatt

You want to succeed in your job? You don't have the time for development seminars, and you don't want to wait until the boss retires to get that promotion?

Many books will tell you that there is no easy path to success and that there is no route to skipping the hard-work part to get you there quickly. They even tell you that the journey is the fun part! All of this is just throwing dust in your eyes to sell you books.

You wanted to find the right book, which shows you the quick path to success? You found it. This book will show you the simplest and best way to boost your career right now. Congratulations!

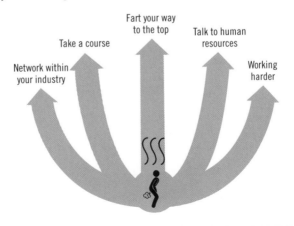

HOW TO DISCREDIT YOUR COLLEAGUES AND BOSS BY FARTING AT WORK

You're on the fast track to success but, as you know, when you do things fast, things can go wrong. Some of your colleagues and a couple of managers will suffer due to your success. Accept it and don't worry about it. Nobody has ever made their way to the top without collateral damage.

Example of strategy

The first person you can discredit in order to take his or her place is your immediate boss, to whom we will refer as #1. But remember, you will need to discredit several people simultaneously to succeed at this. If you discredit your #1 and he or she is fired, it is important to have also discredited all employees who are eligible to take his/her place. The company boss, your #2 (#1's superior) and your #3 (#2's superior) must think that you are the only possible candidate available.

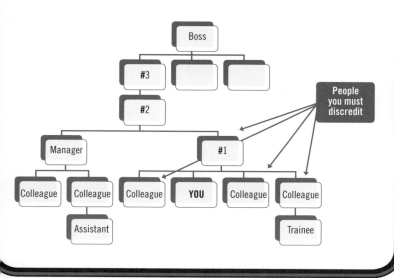

DESTABILIZATION TECHNIQUE #1:
The poisoned mug

Simple to implement, this powerful technique is for use when the employee you want to discredit is on leave. The best thing is that your target will never know he lost credibility during his vacation because of you.

SOLUTION: The generous gift

1. Confirm that the employee you want to discredit has gone on vacation.
2. The day after his departure, enter his office discreetly.
3. Prominently place a mug on his desk with a fart-related inscription. This mug will remain in place during his absence and people who visit his office will not fail to see this incriminating object. Choose an inscription suggesting that he received this mug as a gift from a family member or from one of his closest friends (people who know him well and know who he really is):

I love my dad (even though he farts)
World's best farter... oops father
Fart downloading. Please wait...
I fart. What's your superpower?

4. The day before the end of his holiday go back into his office and remove the mug.

Expert opinion

You can use a fart mug and get good results but be aware that there are many other objects that can discredit your colleague. Examples: a beautiful toilet brush still in its packaging, a pack of toilet deodorizers for "strong odours" or one of these two excellent books — *How to Bonk at Work* or *How to Poo on Holiday.* Guaranteed Results. Remove these objects before he returns.

Testimonial

I successfully used this technique during my boss's holiday to try to take his place. I bought a big black notebook on which I wrote in large capital letters:

MY FART-AT-WORK LOG

I put the notebook in the middle of his office in full view. I filled about thirty pages of the journal, noting the date, time and any "observations". The entries were things like:

"Today, I cannot do it. Seven attempts and nothing but bloating."
"Taco Tuesday = painful cramps for three days."
"Inflammation and pain while sitting. I cancelled the meeting."
"3 farts released during the presentation."
"Abnormal stench."
"I must have a word with the wife tonight."

Pat, 31, paralegal

DESTABILIZATION TECHNIQUE #2:
Farting in a group

This strategy is very simple. You probably already know it and have used it among family or close friends. However, you've probably never dared to use it at work.

SOLUTION: Crowdpooping

1. You are talking to colleagues in a hallway, office or meeting room and need to release some gas.
2. Move your knee slightly to try not to make noise when you break wind.
3. VERY IMPORTANT: you must be the first to ask: "Has something died in here?"
4. Leave immediately, after stating that this is unacceptable and casting an accusing glare at the colleague who is competing with you for your next promotion.
5. It's as simple as that.

Expert opinion

I advise you to wait for the day when your farts smell really bad or search on the Internet for what kinds of food you should combine to get incredibly smelly farts.

Testimonial

There were ten of us at the coffee machine talking business. I accused my colleague Martin. Everyone looked at him disapprovingly. The company boss was there. He asked Martin to go to the bathroom and to come back with some air freshener to disinfect the area he had polluted.

Stephen, 33, magazine editor

To implement this method, you need the person you wish to discredit to be out of the office.

VENI

VIDI

VICI

SOLUTION: The time bomb

1. As soon as the person you want to discredit goes away, sneak quietly into his office without being seen. Once there, release one or two farts. Do this as often as possible.
2. You must ensure that his office windows are closed and that the air conditioning is on the minimum setting.
3. The gas will accumulate in the office and when a colleague or your boss goes in during his absence, they'll find that the room stinks.
4. Your target will soon be known in the company as the employee whose office smells. It is not a great way to get promoted.

Expert opinion

If you do well, in just three or four days the air in the office will become unbreathable. It usually takes only two weeks for the nickname of the employee to become "Stinky Fartman".

Testimonial

I used this method in the office of a colleague. The day he came back, my boss took him to see a doctor to discuss his problem. He also decided that he would no longer go out to meet clients. He is still dealing, but only by phone.

Henry, 43, estate agent

CONCLUSION

Thanks to our sharp observations and Tom Hayatt's erudite advice, your farts at work will never be the same. They will also never again hinder your career development. Now that you have all the knowledge, you are among the best farters in your company. If you dreaded it before, we now hope you will enjoy farting at work.

Here is how your monthly salary should increase in the coming years.

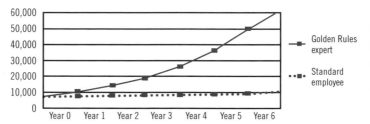

However, based on our thorough observations of the behaviour of people who buy self-improvement books, 98.81% have the disturbing tendency to endlessly accumulate books that are supposed to help them with their career, without ever putting their advice into practice. Gathering theoretical knowledge on a subject without moving on to the practice stage is exactly the same as trying to learn how to drive a car by reading books about cars and driving techniques. It is completely useless.

This book gives you the best information to fart freely, and even fart your way to the top. This is not the kind of self-help book that gives advice on how to dramatically change your life that is impossible to implement. Our techniques are easy. Our readers have been identified as the ones with the fastest salary increases in the world. Our guide has been conceived in a way that allows you to start applying its advice today – and get real benefits from it. Using our techniques to fart at work will significantly increase your salary in coming years! You can trust us on that.

FART AT WORK: Looking for Testimonials

Testimonials from office workers provide the basis for our research. Thanks to them, we can come up with innovative strategies that work in companies. If you lived through one of the following situations, share your experience with the world by sending us your testimonial at matsandenzo@gmail.com. Mention the number of the situation that you are describing in the subject of your e-mail.

1. You were heading to a meeting with your boss. You farted in the corridor, but the odour was following you all the way to his office.
2. You coughed to hide the fart noise, but you didn't synchronize the two very well.
3. Your company installed a water fountain with magnesium-rich water.
4. The cleaning lady suddenly refused to clean your office any longer because it smells too bad.
5. You told your boss: "It was just my phone that vibrated." But he didn't buy it.

6. You said it was the dog by reflex, except you never come to the office with your dog.
7. You opened the window even though it was -10°C outside. Your colleagues wanted to know why.
8. You used the air-freshener spray in the toilet, but you broke the mechanism and the can continued to empty itself for the next four minutes.
9. At the end of a meeting in a foreign country, your nine interlocutors all farted and screamed a word in their language in unison.
10. A cleaning lady left a home-fragrance diffuser in your private office.
11. You noticed your colleagues have been avoiding you. You're beginning to wonder if you hold the title of Mr Fart in the company.
12. You farted in the evening, just before leaving the office. It still smelled the next morning.
13. You read the book *Control Your Farting Through Hypnosis* and wanted to tell everyone about the results you attained with its help.
14. You entered a conference room where a four-hour meeting had just taken place. You would have preferred not to have entered into this tropical vivarium.
15. You farted without knowing that a colleague in a wheelchair was right behind you.
16. A colleague reported you to human resources for your frequent farting. You were summoned to explain.
17. You got a private office. You are the only person in the company to have one. You wonder why.
18. You were flying in business class, sitting next to your boss. You broke wind several times. He soon asked the flight attendant if there was a seat available in the back of the plane, feigning motion sickness.
19. Due to your frequent farting, the human resources department sent you an e-mail to remind you of the company "Rules of Peaceful Co-existence".
20. A colleague suggested you go see his gastroenterologist wife.
21. The company cafeteria ladies have suddenly refused to serve you anything with fibre or legumes.
22. Exercises in cardiac massage during a first-aid course became expulsion exercises.

23. Your Secret Santa gift this year is the book *How to Fart at Work*. Last year, it was *How to Poo at Work*.
24. You had to take part in a yoga course offered by your company.
25. You farted during a group photo shoot in your company. The photo where everyone except you has an expression of disgust on their faces is now gracing the homepage of your company website and different brochures.
26. You farted during a job interview.
27. The start-up you work for has white office chairs. The seat of your chair is starting to turn yellow.
28. Due to your frequent farting, you went to see the company doctor. He came to see you afterwards to explain the results of your exams. You work in an open-plan office.
29. You were in your office kitchenette. A colleague farted 30cm away from you, just as you were opening your lunchbox that your wife had lovingly prepared for you.
30. You farted at work and it was wet.
31. You care for the planet. You e-mailed everyone at the company your recipe for an organic and zero-waste toilet air freshener.
32. Someone left a plan of your building on your desk with all the toilets marked in yellow.
33. You were fired for blatant abuse of flatulence.
34. A colleague once came to spray air deodoriser around you without saying a word.
35. Your boss started talking about creating a fart zone in the building.
36. In an environmentally conscious move, your company decided to begin capturing the methane released by employees in the toilet, and using it as fuel for the gas stoves in the cafeteria.

BFS: FIRST AID – DR SMITH'S ADVICE

It is our legal obligation to acquaint you with some basic first-aid techniques related to farting. Dr Smith will tell us how to help a colleague suffering from the Belly Fart Syndrome (BFS). Together we shall learn the manoeuvres that save lives.

How to quickly help a colleague who is unable to fart

PHASE 1: Gassy lunges

Do the demonstration of the gassy lunge for your colleague. Explain all the stages of this simple yet efficient technique carefully. This is the easiest technique to rapidly release the painful accumulation of stomach gas.

If the gas lunge doesn't work, try this: tell him to lie on his back, ideally on top of his desk. Lift his leg upwards, and then continue pushing it further down until the first flatulence comes out. Repeat as many times as necessary.

PHASE 3: The quintuple expulsion push

If the two previous techniques don't work, your colleague must quickly see your company doctor. He will perform a professional technique (illustrated above): he will press five times on the stomach of your colleague. This deep and gentle push will help your colleague to evacuate his painful flatulence. You can support him by holding his hand.